SNAP

CW01666810

GCSE

History: Medicine and Health in Britain (1000-present)

ALL EXAM BOARDS

Miralo Education Group Ltd owner of SnapRevise® trademark, 96 Drove Road, Weston-Super-Mare, BS23 3NW, United Kingdom

Title: GCSE History Summary Notes: Medicine and Health in Britain
ISBN: 978-1-918046-28-1

Contents

SNAPREVISE

Contents

SNAPREVISE

Timeline of medical developments (1000–present)

SNAPREVISE

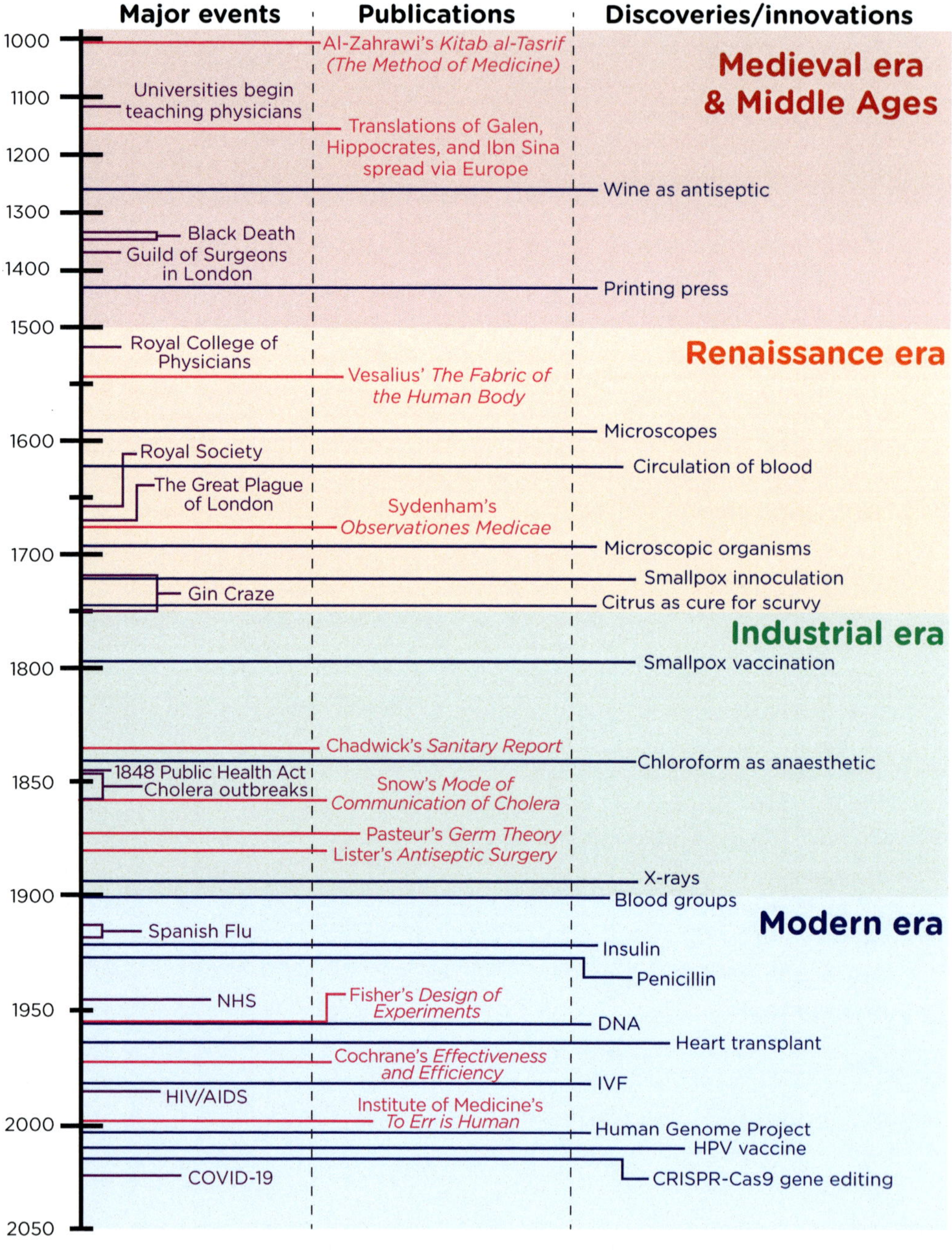

Key individuals in medical history

SNAPREVISE

	Name	Known for
Medieval	Hippocrates	Father of medicine, Theory of Four Humours, Hippocratic Oath
	Galen	Theory of Opposites
	Ibn Sina	Wrote the first medical textbook
	Al-Zahrawi	Founded medical surgery
	Al-Razi	Father of psychology and psychotherapy
	Hugh and Theodoric of Lucca	Wine as antiseptic to treat wounds
	John of Arderne	'Father of English surgery,' treating anal fistulas
Renaissance	Andreas Vesalius	Anatomy and human dissection
	Ambroise Paré	Vascular ligatures, battlefield surgery
	Thomas Sydenham	'English Hippocrates,' clinical observation of patients
	William Harvey	Blood circulation
	John Hunter	Anatomical specimens, dentistry
	Antonie van Leeuwenhoek	Observed bacteria and microorganisms under microscopes
Industrial	Edward Jenner	Vaccination (smallpox)
	Ignaz Semmelweis	Handwashing to reduce maternal mortality
	John Snow	Epidemiology, waterborne cholera transmission
	Louis Pasteur	Germ theory, vaccines, pasteurisation
	Joseph Lister	Antiseptic surgery
	Elizabeth Garrett Anderson	First female doctor
Modern	Florence Nightingale	Founded modern nursing, improved hospital sanitation
	Karl Landsteiner	Blood groups
	Robert Koch	Identified bacteria as causes of disease
	Paul Ehrlich	'Magic bullets,' chemotherapy
	Marie Curie	Radiography, medical imaging
	Alexander Fleming	Discovered penicillin
	Howard Florey and Ernst Chain	Co-developed and mass produced penicillin
	Jonas Salk	Polio vaccine
	Rosalind Franklin	Found evidence of DNA structure
	Tu Youyou	Discovered artemisinin to treat malaria
	Jennifer Doudna and Emmanuelle Charpentier	Co-developed CRISPR gene editing technology

Medieval medicine

Features of medieval Britain

- Most people in medieval Britain lived in **small villages** or **crowded towns** with poor living conditions.
- Houses for the poor were usually made of wood, wattle and daub, with thatched roofs, which were highly flammable and difficult to keep clean.
- Animals were often kept close to or inside homes, increasing the **spread of disease.**
- Diet depended on wealth; the poor mainly ate bread, pottage and vegetables, while the rich consumed meat, fish and spices.
- Clean water was limited, especially in towns, as rivers and wells were often **contaminated** by waste. Cleanliness was a luxury.
- Waste disposal was poor, with human and animal waste frequently thrown into streets or rivers.
- **Public health** was mostly concerned with addressing the **most egregious problems** like contaminated water and rotting rubbish in the streets. For example, fines were issued in the wake of the Black Death in 1350 prohibiting the dumping of "dung and filth of garbage and entrails" into rivers and waterways.
- The Church played a major role in governing people's lives and encouraged ideas of **miraculous healing,** with many shrines containing relics of hair and bones of a holy person.
- Between the years 1000 to 1500, over 700 hospitals were opened.
- The Christian Church controlled universities where people studied medicine and trained to be doctors. However, the Church saw the role of a doctor as a **caretaker and preventer,** providing comfort rather than healing or curing disease.

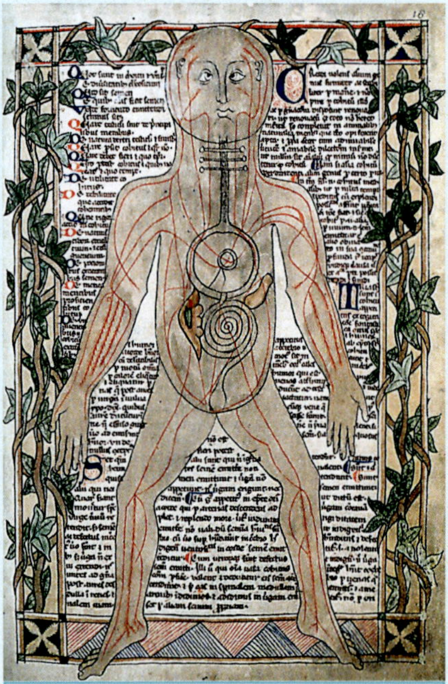

A 13th century anatomical illustration (~1292)

Medieval explanations for illness

- **Religious explanations:**
    - There was a strong belief that sickness came from God as a **punishment**, and so curing an illness was perceived as a challenge to God. Instead, experiencing illness was a way to cleanse the soul.
    - The Church dominated education and medical training, so people believed what priests told them about illness. Dissections were discouraged by the Church, so understanding of anatomy was poor.
- **Miasma:**
    - People believed that **bad air** (miasma, Greek word for pollution) from rotting matter and dirt caused disease, since they had no knowledge of bacteria.
    - This idea came from Hippocrates' book *Airs, Waters, and Places.*
- **Astrology:**
    - Some believed the alignment of planets and stars (astrology) had an effect on illness, so physicians consulted star charts for diagnoses.
    - Although disliked by the Church, astrology and soothsayers gained popularity in the Black Death as people were desperate for answers.
- **The Four Humours:**
    - The theory that the human body was made up of four elements: blood, black bile, yellow bile, and phlegm.
    - It was believed that a person became ill when one of the humours was out of balance, and it was the doctor's job to rebalance these.
    - The theory was created by Hippocrates and later developed by Galen with the Theory of Opposites. Galen suggested treating an illness with an excess of one humour with its opposite (e.g. eating hot peppers to treat an excess of cold phlegm).
    - The humours were linked to seasons, elements, and phases of life.

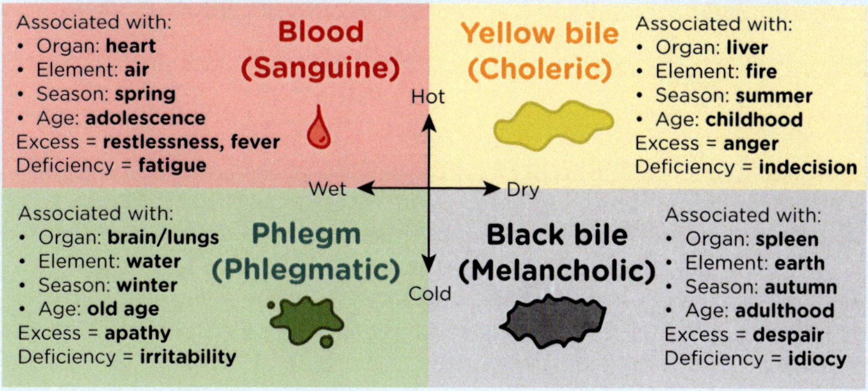

Medieval cures and prevention

- **Religious methods:** praying, fasting, going on pilgrimages, and flagellation (whipping oneself to seek God's forgiveness).
- **Humoural treatments:** involved trying to balance the Four Humours.
  - **Purging:** patients were given emetics (to make them vomit) and empty their bowels to clear out their systems. Some apothecaries even gave their patients poison.
  - **Bloodletting:** involved using leeches, cupping, or cutting a vein to drain out an 'imbalance' of blood.
  - **Herbal remedies:** patients were given spice-based mixtures to drink, smell, or bathe in to clear out blockages and remove 'miasma.'
- **Astrology:** star charts and almanacs (books about astronomical and meteorological events) were used since astrology was believed to affect health, with planets thought to influence different parts of the body.
- **Miasma prevention:** people carried sweet-smelling herbs and flowers or burnt pleasant-smelling substances to purify the air.
- **Regimen sanitatis:** a famous poem containing advice on healthy living, such as diet, exercise, and hygiene, to avoid illness.

Medieval doctors and medical professionals

- **Physicians:** university-trained for seven years, expected to provide diagnoses (limited to taking pulses and examining the colour, smell, and taste of urine). They learnt mainly by listening to lectures and debating ideas, often graduating without ever seeing a patient. They were the highest status medical practitioners and were very expensive.
- **Apothecaries:** mixed and sold herbal remedies, including poisons. They were disliked by physicians as they offered much cheaper treatments.
- **Barber surgeons:** were lower-class medics who could perform basic surgery by learning through experience. Common procedures included:
  - **Bloodletting:** making a small cut on the inside of the arms and letting 'excess' blood drain out in order to balance the humours.
  - **Amputation:** removing a painful or infected part of the body.
  - **Cauterisation:** a very painful method of burning a wound to stop the blood flow, done with a heated iron.
  - **Drilling:** some conditions like epilepsy were believed to be caused by demons in the brain, so a surgeon would drill a hole into the skull.
- **Women:** cared for the sick at home but couldn't become doctors.

Profile: Hippocrates

Hippocrates
(b. ~460 BCE, d. ~375 BCE)

- Hippocrates was an ancient Greek doctor often described as the **'Father of Medicine.'**
- He believed that diseases had **natural causes** rather than being sent by God as punishment.
- Hippocrates developed the **Theory of the Four Humours**, which stated that health depended on a balance of blood, phlegm, black bile, and yellow bile.
- He also established the **Hippocratic Oath,** a set of ethical guidelines for doctors.
- Hippocratic treatments focused on restoring balance through diet, exercise, and bloodletting.
- His ideas represented an important early move away from supernatural explanations, although Hippocrates' work was limited by a lack of scientific knowledge and technology and adherence to his ideas stifled progress for centuries.

Profile: Galen

Galen
(b. 129 CE, d. 216 CE)

- Galen was a physician whose ideas dominated European medicine for 1,400 years.
- He expanded Hippocrates' Theory of the Four Humours and developed the **Theory of Opposites** about how to balance the humours.
- Like Hippocrates, Galen prescribed treatments such as purging and bloodletting.
- He was also an advocate for animal dissections as a means of learning about anatomy, as human dissection was banned in Ancient Rome.
- His work was highly respected because it aligned with Christian beliefs and was supported by the Church. However, Galen's ideas also acted as a barrier to progress because they discouraged questioning and experimentation even though some of his findings were incorrect; for example, he thought blood was made in the liver.

Medieval medicine

Profile: Abu Bakr al-Razi (Rhazes)

- Al-Razi was a leading Persian physician who made important advances in clinical medicine and wrote over 150 books on the subject.
- He was one of the first doctors to clearly distinguish between **smallpox and measles.**
- Al-Razi prioritised observation, experimentation, and recording symptoms. He supported hospital-based care and believed doctors should rely on **evidence** rather than authority.
- He was a follower of Galen but actively challenged many of his ideas; one of his books was called 'Doubts about Galen.'
- His work encouraged a more **scientific approach** to medicine and set the foundations for psychology, though it spread slowly to Europe.

Abu Bakr al-Razi
(b. ~864 d. ~925)

Profile: Ibn Sina (Avicenna)

- Ibn Sina was a Persian physician whose medical knowledge had a major influence on medieval Europe.
- He wrote **The Canon of Medicine**, which became a standard medical textbook for centuries.
    - It contained information on 760 drugs, and problems such as obesity and anorexia.
    - The first Latin translation of the Canon of Medicine appeared in the twelfth century. Top universities in Italy soon started using these books to teach medicine.
- Ibn Sina supported the Theory of the Four Humours but also emphasised careful diagnosis and observation.
- His work preserved and developed ancient Greek medical knowledge during the Islamic Golden Age.
- Islamic views on illness differed to that of Christianity at the time: Islam encouraged medical learning, with followers being taught **'For every disease, God has given a cure.'**
- The Canon improved medical education but also reinforced traditional ideas that limited progress.

Ibn Sina
(b. ~980 d.1037)

Profile: Hugh of Lucca and Theodoric of Lucca

***Hugh of Lucca** (b. 1160 d. ~1256) and **Theodoric of Lucca** (b. 1205 d. ~1296)*

- Hugh of Lucca was a medieval Italian surgeon who challenged traditional ideas about **wound treatment.** His son, Theodoric of Lucca, recorded and spread these ideas through medical texts.
- Hugh rejected the belief that pus was a sign of healing and instead promoted cleaning wounds thoroughly. He encouraged the use of **clean dressings** and **careful wound management.**
- Their 1267 book criticised the common view that pus was needed to heal a wound, instead recommending the use of **wine** on wounds to speed up healing and prevent infections.
- Despite being ahead of their time in methods of **reducing infection,** their ideas contradicted Hippocratic and Galenic teachings so did not become popular.

Profile: John of Arderne

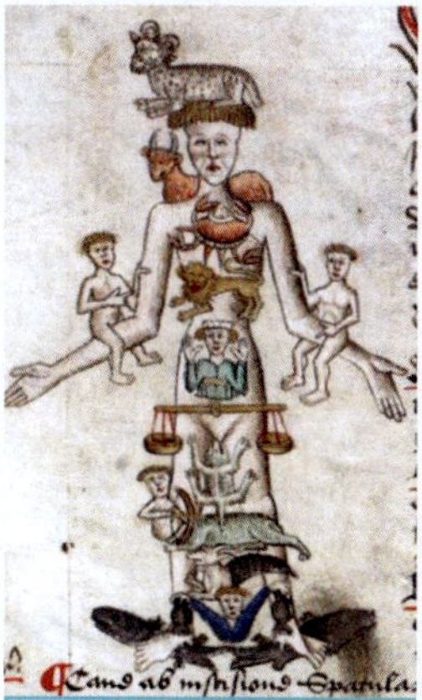

John of Arderne
(b. 1307 d. 1392)
a medical drawing of astrological/zodiac signs and associated organs

- John of Arderne was a medieval English surgeon who made important advances in surgical practice.
- He is best known for developing treatments for anal fistulas, a condition common among knights. He charged large fees to treat these abscesses in knights.
- Arderne emphasised practical experience and careful observation rather than blind reliance on ancient texts. His illustrations were based on Greek and Arab knowledge during the Hundred Years War.
- He believed in pain relief and used opium-based anaesthetics to reduce suffering during surgery. His work helped improve the reputation of surgeons, who were often viewed as inferior to physicians.
- He tried to separate surgeons from lower-class barbers by forming The Guild of Surgeons in the City of London in 1368.

Medieval hospitals

- Most hospitals were **run by the Church** as caring for the sick was seen as a religious duty. These were staffed by **monks and nuns** who could provide food and beds (often shared).
- Hospitals rarely had doctors and treatments largely consisted of **herbal remedies and prayer.**
- There were approximately **1,200 hospitals** in England and Wales.
- **St. Mary of Bethlehem (Bedlam)** was a famous hospital for the "poor or silly persons" (people with mental illness).
- Insane, contagious, and pregnant patients were usually not admitted.
- Some hospitals called **lazar houses** specialised in caring for **lepers** and quarantine them since leprosy was known to be contagious.
- **Surgery** was typically a last resort, due to the problem of shock and pain. Techniques were basic and dangerous due to lack of anaesthetics and antiseptics. Some attempts were made to put the patient to sleep using **hemlock** or **opium**, but typically would require holding or tying the patient down.

Medieval public health

- Medieval towns were built near **rivers** for easier access to water and transport. However, many people through their waste into the streets, which would travel into the water system.
- Most towns had **privies** with **cesspits** underneath to collect sewage. These were dug out annually by gong farmers.
- Some town councils tried to keep the environment clean, passing local laws encouraging people to remove their rubbish, but this was difficult to enforce. For example, in 1388, a £20 fine was introduced for throwing 'dung garbage'.
- **Christian monasteries and abbeys** were often situated in isolated areas, but still close to rivers with piping and filtering systems to deliver pure water.
    - The isolation and religious routines of cleanliness helped to protect monks from epidemics, such as the plague.
    - These were very wealthy buildings, as many people gave money and donations, allowing monks to build good sanitation facilities.
    - Monks were educated, had access to books, bathed often, and lived fairly isolated lives. The sanitation and monks' knowledge meant conditions were better in these areas.

The Black Death (1346–1353)

- The **Black Death** was an outbreak of the **bubonic (swollen lymph nodes) and pneumonic (affecting the lungs and breathing) plague**.
- It killed about **one-third to one-half** of the British population after arriving in Weymouth.
- Victims often died within **three to four days.**
- It was spread by fleas and infected droplets, and the main symptoms were pus-filled buboes. Since no one could cure the plague, treatments often focused on dealing with buboes.

Beliefs about causes	Prevention methods	Treatments	Consequences
• **Punishment from God** for mankind's sins • Extreme imbalance of the **four humours** • **Astrology:** unusual positions of Mars, Jupiter, and Saturn • **Miasma:** bad air from decaying rubbish or poisonous gases from volcanoes • **Outsiders:** strangers or witches blamed for causing disease; Jewish people blamed for poisoning wells	• **Prayer, fasting,** and **pilgrimages** • **Flagellants** whipped themselves to ask for God's forgiveness • **Lighting fires** and carrying **sweet herbs and spices** to clean the air • **Quarantine**: houses with sick people were shut for 40 days (largely ineffective as local authorities had limited power)	• **Prayer, confessing sins** (or accepting the plague as God's will) • **Bloodletting** • **Purging** • Some physicians advised **plucking a chicken** and holding its skin on the buboes (believing that skin was permeable so the miasma would be transferred from the patient to the chicken)	◦ **Food shortages:** lords pivoted from crops to sheep farming as it required fewer workers, causing inflation of basic foods like bread. ◦ **Peasant wages:** some peasants who survived believed they were divinely protected and demanded higher wages. ◦ **Religious changes:** many priests died from the plague, and those who deserted were criticised for their cowardice. This meant the church suffered a **loss of reputation** as well as a **loss of clergy.** ◦ **Prejudices:** due to misunderstandings about where the Black Death came from, there was widespread persecution of **foreigners, beggars,** and **lepers.**

Renaissance medicine

Features of Renaissance Britain

- The **Renaissance** (c.1500–c.1700) was a period of **"rebirth"** in Europe, where people started to question old ideas and focus more on **observation and experimentation**. This was a time of huge change in arts and sciences. In medicine, people started to question medieval ideas of Galen and Hippocrates and make new discoveries.
- Renaissance thinking increasingly emphasised **observation, experimentation and scientific investigation.**
- **Consequences of the Renaissance** included:
    - **New inventions:** technology such as gunpowder meant a new type of wound for soldiers. Doctors had to find new ways to deal with illness and injury.
    - **New lands:** sailors used more accurate mapping techniques, bringing back new medicines from their travels.
    - **New art:** more realist drawings and techniques emerged, enabling artists like Michelangelo to study the body in more detail, improving anatomical knowledge.
    - **New ideas:** the printing press allowed ideas to spread quickly across Europe. In addition, updated scientific methods including observation, hypotheses, and experimentation led to the questioning of old beliefs.
- **Urban overcrowding** increased, particularly among the poor, leading to the rapid spread of disease.
- **Diet** varied greatly by wealth; the poor continued to rely on bread and cheap food, while the rich had more varied diets.
- **Clean water supplies** remained limited, with rivers and wells often contaminated by waste. **Waste disposal** improved slowly, but many towns still relied on open drains, cesspits, and dumping waste into streets.
- Cheap gin led to **widespread alcoholism,** particularly among the urban poor. This was known as the **Gin Craze** (1720–1751). The government passed several Gin Acts to restrict the sale and production of gin, aiming to reduce crime and disorder.

A 17th century colourised engraving of a plague doctor

Renaissance explanations for illness

- Medical understanding during the Renaissance showed strong continuity with medieval ideas rather than major change. The **Theory of the Four Humours** and **miasma theory** remained dominant.
- **Religious explanations** also remained influential, with many people believing disease was sent by God as punishment or a test of faith, but it became less common to assume diseases had supernatural causes as gradually a more scientific approach evolved.
- Scientists and physicians could rely on **new methods** of diagnosis and treatment beyond the medieval urine analysis.
- **The Royal Society** (founded 1660) was a group for scientists and doctors to share and publish new ideas, supported by King Charles II. They explored new ideas such as:
    - **Animacules:** the idea that tiny animals (now known as microbes) caused disease was proven through observations under early microscopes, though these were not powerful enough to identify microorganisms until the late 1600s.
    - **Transference:** some believed disease could be transferred to objects or animals.
- People began to look for chemical cures and noticed that weather and **environmental factors** might affect disease.
- Hospitals started to treat a wider range of illnesses, and some **specialised** in certain diseases.

Renaissance cures and prevention

- Many old methods continued: **bloodletting, purging, herbal remedies, regimen sanitatis,** and **miasma prevention.**
- Medical treatments still depended on what people could afford.
- Discoveries of new lands brought back new, natural medicines such as **lemons and limes** to treat scurvy, and **opium** from Turkey as an anaesthetic. **Tobacco** from North America was also initially thought to cure disease.
- Local and national governments started to take more responsibility for public health through **urban improvements** like paving streets, improving drainage, and removing waste, thus reducing 'miasma' and improving air quality.

Renaissance medicine

Renaissance doctors and medical professionals

- **Physicians** remained university-trained and focused on diagnosis.
- **Barber surgeons:** still a common choice for small operations like bloodletting for those who couldn't afford physicians. However, surgeons became more respected due to improved training and scientific approaches.
- **Apothecaries:** still had little to no medical training, but sold a wider range of herbs and medicines.
- **Quacks:** travelling tradesmen who sold 'cure-alls' which were fake cures that exploited people's fear of disease. They typically put on a show to attract patients.
- **Wise women:** used superstition to diagnose and cure illnesses through plants and herbs.
- **Women:** still cared for the sick at home.

Profile: Andreas Vesalius

Andreas van Wezel
(b. 1514 d. 1564)

- Vesalius was a professor of surgery in Padua, Italy. He was initially a key follower of Galen's theories, but later questioned and opposed them.
- Unusually for the time, he conducted his own **dissections**, rather than leaving it to an assistant.
- Galen's work was often based on animal dissections, rather than human, so Vesalius also dissected animals to evaluate Galen's knowledge and correct some of his mistakes. For example, a human breastbone had three parts, not seven like an ape.
- Vesalius' findings were made available to scholars and barber-surgeons in his illustrated textbook ***The Fabric of the Human Body.*** Unlike other books that focused on individual organs, Vesalius focused on how different systems worked within the body.
- He encouraged other doctors to do their own dissections, inspiring others like Fabricus who discovered valves in veins.
- Vesalius' work **overturned centuries of belief** that Galen's ideas of anatomy were correct. Whilst it did not lead to any new cures, it established a new basis for an understanding of the human body and made anatomy central to medical study.

Profile: Ambroise Paré

Ambroise Paré
(b. 1510 d. 1590)

- Paré was a French surgeon who worked on the battlefields during the Battle of Milan in 1536.
- He published several books about his work **making surgery safer** and less painful, though infection was still a major problem.
- Paré translated Latin works into French, increasing others' understanding of **anatomy**, since most surgeons did not learn Latin.
- His books soon circulated across Europe. An English handwritten translation of his work was given to the Barber-Surgeons of London in 1591 long before it was printed in English in 1634.
- Some of Paré's innovations were:
  - **Treating gunshots:** surgeons previously believed gunshots were poisonous so used burning oil to remove the 'poison' and then apply a soothing cream. When Paré ran out of oil, he used rose oil, egg white, and turpentine which was a better ointment for wounds.
  - **Vascular ligature:** instead of cauterising (burning) wounds with a red-hot iron, Paré used ligatures (thread) to tie off blood vessels and stop bleeding during surgery. He also designed the **beak's clamp** to halt bleeding whilst the vessels were being tied.
  - **False limbs:** due to the speed of amputations required on the battlefield, Paré designed his own limbs for wounded soldiers as an early form of prosthetic.

Profile: Thomas Sydenham

Thomas Sydenham
(b. 1624 d. 1689)

- Sydenham worked as a doctor in London and was nicknamed the **'English Hippocrates'** because he focused on carefully **observing patients.**
- He believed diseases were like different types of animals that could be grouped together.
- His book *Observationes Medicae* (1676) described his theories and his belief in treating the whole disease, not just symptoms.
- He did not rely on established ideas of medicine and instead prioritised his own observations of patients.
- He was the first to distinguish between measles and scarlet fever.

SNAPREVISE

Profile: William Harvey

William Harvey
(b. 1578 d. 1657)

- Harvey challenged Galen's ideas that blood was made in the liver and used as a fuel that was burned in the body.
- He demonstrated that **blood circulates continuously** around the body in a closed system, rather than being constantly produced and used up (although he could not explain why blood needed to circulate).
- He studied **human hearts** and dissected the hearts of cold-blooded animals to understand how muscles worked.
- He discovered the **circulation of blood** and proved that **arteries and veins** were one connected system. He also theorised that blood moves between arteries and veins through tiny passages (which today we know as capillaries).
- Harvey experimented by trying to pump blood the wrong way around, proving that **blood could only go one way.**
- He mathematically worked out how much blood would have been needed if it was produced as fuel for the body. By **estimating blood volume and heart output,** he proved that Galen's model (blood being consumed by organs) was mathematically impossible
- However, he could not explain how the blood moved from arteries to veins (as microscopes at the time weren't powerful enough to view capillaries).
- Early experiments based on his ideas sometimes led to deaths due to shock or wrong blood types.
- He knew that if he were right, he would be challenging medical ideas of humours and bloodletting, so his ideas were slow to be accepted.
- Harvey's work was published in 1628, and the immediate response was critical. Some doctors rejected his ideas for contradicting Galen, and many viewed him as a quack. It took another 50 years before the University of Paris taught his findings to students.
- Harvey's discovery was not immediately useful, but in the long term, the circulation of blood was key to understanding modern medicine, conditions like diabetes or heart disease, and innovations like blood tests.

Profile: John Hunter

John Hunter
(b. 1728 d.1793)

- John Hunter was a Scottish surgeon and highly distinguished physician and researcher.
- At the age of 20, Hunter joined his brother's anatomy school where he began a large collection of 3000 stuffed or dried **body parts, plants and fossils.** He used his collection to experiment with inflating narrow blood vessels.
- In 1785, when a man entered the hospital with an aneurysm above the knee, Hunter challenged the usual treatments. Rather than amputating the leg, Hunter cut at several points of the leg and tied his arteries together to restrict his blood flow above the aneurysm. Six weeks later, the patient was able to walk again.
- He even experimented on himself by injecting himself with gonorrhoea pus to test if two diseases could exist in the same organ. Unbeknownst to him, the patient also had syphilis, infecting Hunter with two diseases.
- Many surgeons whom Hunter trained became great medical professionals (e.g. Edward Jenner, who invented vaccinations).
- Hunter's **willingness to experiment** was key to his success as a surgeon, and his writings were an important contribution to surgical work and helped to make other discoveries.

Profile: Antonie van Leeuwenhoek

Antonie van Leeuwenhoek
(b. 1632 d.1723)

- van Leeuwenhoek was the first person to observe and describe **microorganisms** using **microscopes** he designed himself.
- He discovered **bacteria, protozoa, sperm cells,** and **red blood cells.**
- His observations laid the foundations of **microbiology** as a scientific discipline, providing crucial early evidence that living organisms could exist beyond human sight.
- His work challenged existing medical beliefs that were based on limited anatomical knowledge.
- Later scientists, including Pasteur and Koch in the industrial era, built directly on his discoveries in developing germ theory and modern understanding of disease transmission.

Renaissance medicine

Renaissance public health

- Renaissance public health measures were generally **reactive rather than preventative** and were limited by their continued reliance on miasma theory. One exception was the development of inoculation and later vaccination methods towards the end of the 1700s.
- **Inoculation** works by giving healthy people a mild form of illness from an infected person, building up their resistance to the disease. It was already relatively popular in Asia during the 1500s.
- In 1721, **smallpox** inoculation became popular in Britain after an aristocrat inoculated her children, having seen it done in Turkey.
- Edward Jenner had heard theories that milkmaids who caught **cowpox** were **protected against smallpox** and tested this by injecting cowpox into an eight-year-old boy, then inoculating him with smallpox eight weeks later. The boy did not react to the inoculation, leading to Jenner's discovery of **vaccination** (from the Latin word for cow, vacca).
- However, Jenner could not explain why vaccination worked, making it difficult for others to accept it. Many doctors profited from inoculation so disliked Jenner's new discovery even though it was safer.
- Although others had made similar discoveries, Jenner was the first to use scientific testing methods. By 1853, Britain had made smallpox vaccination compulsory, and it was completely eradicated in 1980.

Renaissance hospitals

- When King Henry VIII broke away from the Catholic Church, he closed down monasteries, so care was increasingly funded by **charitable donations** rather than religious institutions.
- In the 1700s, hospitals were places where the **sick were cured** but also often had attached **medical schools** where doctors received training.
- Doctors gained official posts in hospitals, developing their reputation and attracting wealthier patients. They saw ordinary patients for free, but fees paid by **private patients** were their main source of income.
- Towards the end of the eighteenth century, hospitals added **public dispensaries** to provide free medicine for the poor.
- This period also saw the opening of more specialist hospitals such as:
  - Bethlem Hospital (1634) for the mentally ill
  - London Lock Hospital (1746) for venereal diseases
  - Middlesex Maternity Hospital (1745)
  - Foundling Hospital (1741) for orphaned children

The Great Plague (1665–1666)

- The Great Plague of London killed approximately 100,000 people (15% of London's population).
- Like the Black Death, this was a bubonic plague characterised by buboes, swelling, fever, and high mortality.
- Many medieval beliefs about miasma or divine punishment being the cause of plague still persisted. In reality, the plague was spread by fleas which lived on rats.
- Unlike the Black Death, local authorities had a more organised approach which meant fewer deaths and more chances at prevention. This marked the beginning of a greater understanding of the importance of hygiene, and distancing.

Beliefs about causes	Prevention methods	Treatments	Consequences
• Punishment from God • Astrological events • Miasma • Imbalance of humours • Person-to-person contact	• Smoking to keep away the poisoned air • Carrying pomanders (sweet-smelling objects) • Smelling a sponge soaked with vinegar to cleanse out the bad smells • If you were rich enough, moving to the countryside to avoid catching it	• Bleeding with leeches • Prayers and fasting to atone for sins • Paid 'women searchers' to examine the sick and note those with symptoms • Plague victims were quarantined with watchmen • Houses painted with red crosses and words 'Lord Have Mercy on Us' • Bodies were brought out at night to avoid contamination	• Local authorities banned public gatherings, cleaned streets, killed stray animals believed to spread the disease, and burned tar and herbs to cleanse the air • The border with Scotland was closed, and trade between towns was stopped • Plague doctors wore bird-like masks filled with scents like flowers

Features of industrial Britain

- The Industrial Revolution took place in the 18th and 19th centuries. The **population doubled** during this time and **technology rapidly advanced.**
- **Industrialisation** led to rapid population growth in towns and cities such as Manchester, Birmingham, and Leeds. Migration from rural areas was common since factory work offered regular wages, and agricultural mechanisation reduced rural employment. However, this meant cities expanded too quickly for infrastructure to cope.
- Workers lived in **overcrowded, poorly built** housing (often back-to-back terraced houses that lacked ventilation and running water). This overcrowding increased the spread of disease.
- Towns grew very quickly in the 1800s as people flocked to new jobs in factories. For example, the population of Sheffield in 1750 was 12,000, and by 1850 this had grown to 150,000.
- Few houses had toilets; some had buckets in the corner of their room that would be emptied into the street or stored until there was enough to sell as manure. Street toilets were a deep hole with a wooden shed over it, shared with many families.
- Water came from pumps that connected to filthy rivers and ponds.
- Diets were poor, especially for the working class. Food was often adulterated (e.g. chalk in flour, water in milk), and **malnutrition** weakened immune systems.
- Water was often taken from rivers contaminated with sewage, or from shared water pumps which increased infection risk.
- Human waste was stored in cesspits which frequently overflowed. Industrial waste from factories also began to further pollute water sources.
- Early nineteenth-century governments believed in **laissez-faire** (non-interventionist) attitudes, so responsibility for health was seen as an individual issue.

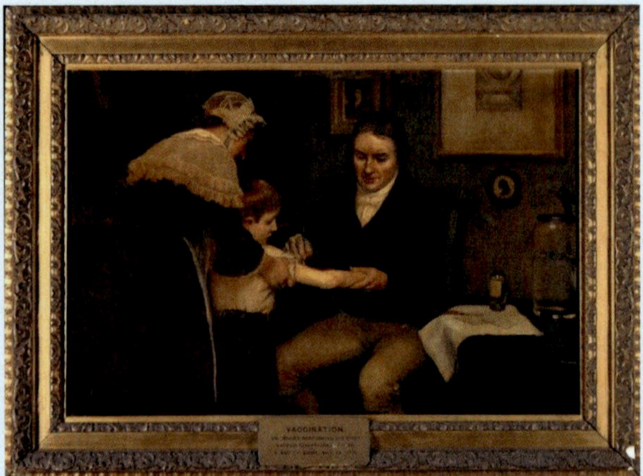

A 1910 painting by Ernest Board of Edward Jenner performing his first vaccination on 8-year-old James Phipps in 1796

Industrial cures and preventions

- Early industrial-era cures were largely ineffective and based on traditional ideas. Gradual improvements included **vaccination against smallpox** and **improved sanitation** reducing disease spread.
- Germ theory led to more effective treatments and preventative measures.
- **Prevention** became more important than cure by the late nineteenth century.
- The most common diseases of the time included typhoid, tuberculosis (TB), and cholera.

Industrial era explanations for illness

- Miasma theory was still widely accepted by doctors, the government, and the public because:
    - It fit what people could see and smell (filthy streets, bad odours).
    - It explained why disease was associated with poverty and overcrowded areas.
    - It did not challenge religious beliefs.
- Another common belief was **spontaneous generation** – the theory that illness appeared randomly when something rotted. People initially believed disease was caused by microbes, rather than the other way around.
- Some continuity from earlier periods remained in **religious explanations**, especially among the poor, who believed disease was a punishment from God.
- Towards the 19th century, people began to question these theories and the idea of **specificity** (i.e. not all microbes were the same and each caused a specific illness).
- This gave rise to **germ theory** which states that microscopic **pathogens ('germs') cause disease**.
- There was gradual change in understandings of medicine throughout this period due to:
    - Advances in science and technology
    - Improvements in microscopes
    - Increased use of experimentation
- However, some revolutionary ideas were slow to catch on because they challenged long-standing beliefs, and because some early forms of technology made proof difficult.

Industrial doctors and medical professionals

- Medical professionals during this period increasingly focused on understanding the links between **environment, disease, and public health** due to urbanisation and overcrowding. They also relied more on **observation, statistics, and experimentation** rather than tradition.
- Surgeons improved techniques through better understandings of **anatomy, anaesthesia, and antiseptics.**
- The **Medical Act of 1858** resulted in higher standards of training in medical schools, hospital-based learning, and formal qualifications from universities.
- Both hospital procedures and medical education became more structured, reflecting a trend toward **professionalisation** and **standardisation** in medicine.
- Public health reformers worked with governments to improve water supply and sewage systems, particularly in response to cholera outbreaks.
- There was a shift in focus from individual treatment to **population-wide prevention methods.**

Profile: Edward Jenner

Edward Jenner
(b. 1749 d. 1823)

- Jenner was an English doctor who developed the world's **first successful vaccination.**
- Jenner was a surgeon apprentice from age 13-19 and then went on to study in London with John Hunter who encouraged him to conduct his own experiments and develop hypotheses.
- In 1796, Jenner discovered that exposure to **cowpox** could protect people from **smallpox**, testing his theory through experimentation and publishing his findings in 1798.
- Vaccination represented a major new approach to prevention rather than cure, as vaccination was safer and more effective than inoculation.
- Although his ideas faced opposition, vaccination became increasingly widespread and was made compulsory in Britain in 1853.
- Jenner's work laid the foundations for modern immunisation programmes.

Profile: Louis Pasteur

Louis Pasteur
(b. 1822 d. 1895)

- Pasteur was a French chemist who developed **germ theory** which proved that microorganisms cause disease, and **disproved the theory of spontaneous generation.** He also developed ideas on vaccination and pasteurisation.
- **Vaccination:**
    - In 1880, Pasteur was investigating chicken cholera. His assistant, Charles Chamberlain, accidentally left the petri dish out for four days, and when Pasteur tested it on animals, the chickens never died. This led to the development of the **chicken cholera vaccine.**
    - Pasteur later developed vaccines for anthrax and rabies, building on the work of Edward Jenner.
- However, his ideas were not immediately accepted. Most doctors did not believe microscopic germs could harm a human. Germ theory was first considered by vets in the UK before it became consensus among doctors.
- **Pasteurisation:**
    - From 1857 to 1860, he investigated why milk and wine went sour. He discovered that if air was kept out of the swan's neck flask, then the liquid would not sour.
    - Pasteur identified the microbe responsible for souring wine and showed that heating it to a specific temperature would kill the microbes and so it would not go off. He thus correctly concluded that **bacteria and germs** were responsible for souring milk and wine.
    - Pasteur's work would later inspire Joseph Lister in developing antiseptics.

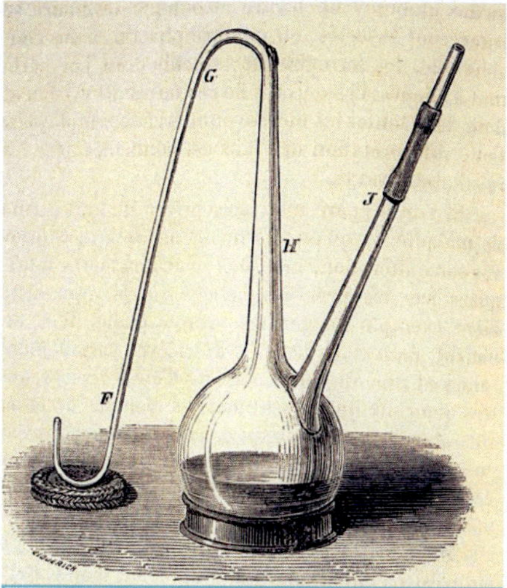

A sketch of a 'swan-neck' flask used by Pasteur in his experiments to disprove spontaneous generation

SNAPREVISE

Profile: Joseph Lister

- Lister was a surgeon and pathologist who studied bacteria and developed **antiseptic techniques** to make surgery safer.
- Lister believed that infections only happened when the skin was broken.
- When seeing a patient with a fractured leg, he decided to soak the leg in **carbolic acid** instead of amputating, and he found the boy's leg healed well.

Joseph Lister
(b. 1827 d. 1912)

Profile: John Snow

- Snow theorised that disease was not caused by miasma, but **dirty water.**
- He created a map showing cholera deaths in his local area, noting that they all seemed to be centred around the Broad Street Pump. He removed the pump, and quickly, deaths decreased.
- Snow presented his findings to parliament, proving that cholera was spread by contaminated water, and suggesting a new sewer system be developed to prevent spread.
- Overall, Snow had an immediate impact on the Broad Street area, but his impact outside of this area was limited, and the significance of his **epidemiology** (studying the spread of a disease) would not be understood until later.
- His work wasn't initially taken seriously due to a lack of germ theory proof. The Great Stink later motivated Parliament to act and build a sewage system, acknowledging Snow's findings.

John Snow
(b. 1813 d. 1858)

A map of incidence of cholera clustered around the Broad Street water pump

Profile: Robert Koch

Robert Koch
(b. 1843 d. 1910)

- Koch was a German microbiologist and expanded Pasteur's germ theory and the field of bacteriology. He identified bacteria that caused **cholera, anthrax,** and **TB.**
- Pasteur and Koch were rivals competing for the next breakthrough in vaccinations. There were several factors that contributed to this:
    - **War:** the rivalry between the two increased after France lost a war against Germany. Armies could lose more men to illness, which meant racing to find cures.
    - **Individuality:** Pasteur was a hard-working scientist despite losing his daughter to typhoid and having a stroke. Koch was also a rigorous scientist who pushed to discover more each time.
    - **Communication:** after making his discovery, Pasteur demonstrated his vaccine in front of audiences in France. News was quickly spread through the electric telegraph.

Profile: Paul Ehrlich

Paul Ehrlich
(b. 1854 d. 1915)

- Ehrlich was a German scientist developed the idea of **'magic bullets'** - chemicals targeting specific disease-causing microbes without harming the rest of the body.
- In 1909, Ehrlich created **Salvarsan 606**, the first effective treatment for syphilis, which had previously been widespread and often fatal. Ehrlich worked with his colleague Sahachiro Hata tested over 600 compounds before finding a successful one.
- His work marked a major change in medicine away from general remedies towards targeted, scientific drugs and chemotherapy.

Profile: Elizabeth Garrett Anderson

Elizabeth Garrett Anderson
(b. 1836 d. 1917)

- Anderson was a **pioneer for women** in medicine during the 19th century. She faced significant legal and social barriers, as women were not allowed to qualify as doctors in the UK.
- Anderson overcame these obstacles by qualifying through the Society of Apothecaries in 1865. She became the **first woman** to be officially recognised as a doctor in Britain.
- She founded the **New Hospital for Women** in London, staffed entirely by women who would treat female patients.

Industrial hospitals

- During the nineteenth century, many hospitals were funded through endowments (known as endowed hospitals) provided by **wealthy individuals, charities, and religious organisations** rather than by the government. Endowed hospitals represented a significant change from earlier periods, as they aimed to provide **organised medical care** rather than simply housing the sick.
- They became more **accessible to the poor,** who previously relied on home remedies or parish support, although admission was often restricted to the **'deserving poor.'**
- Funding from donors allowed hospitals to expand in size, employ trained staff, and invest in better facilities. Hospitals gradually became cleaner with better systems of hygiene, ventilation, and waste disposal.
- Hospitals increasingly separated patients into different wards according to illness or severity, which helped to limit the spread of infection.
- The introduction of **anaesthetics** in the mid-nineteenth century marked a major turning point in surgery as they reduced pain for patients, allowing surgeons to operate more carefully and attempt longer, more complex procedures.
    - **Ether** was one of the first anaesthetics used, but it was unpleasant and difficult to administer.
    - Thomas Beddoes experimented with **nitrous oxide** (laughing gas), noting how it made him feel giddy and relaxed, but not recognising its medical value.
    - James Simpson promoted the use of **chloroform**, which was more effective and easier to use during operations.
        - In 1847, Simpson and his friends were testing different substances at a party when someone knocked over a bottle of chloroform. Simpson's wife brought them dinner and found them all asleep.
        - Simpson then tested chloroform on himself as a potential anaesthetic to reduce pain during surgery.
        - Chloroform was especially popular as an aid to childbirth, used by Queen Victoria and Emma Darwin (wife of Charles Darwin).
- Despite major advances, surgery remained dangerous for much of the nineteenth century. **Severe bleeding** was still a major risk because effective methods to control blood loss were limited. **Infection**, although reduced by antiseptic and aseptic techniques, continued to be a threat until these methods became widely accepted and consistently used.

Industrial public health

- Social reformer Edwin Chadwick wrote a report on living conditions shocked Britain. Over 10,000 copies were handed to politicians, and 20,000 sold directly to the public. His report directly led to the **Public Health Act 1848** and the government taking responsibility for people's health (though the reforms Chadwick suggested weren't made compulsory so changes were limited at first).
- This would be followed by the **Public Health Act 1875** following the Great Stink of excessive sewage in the Thames which required cities to provide clean water to its citizens and dispose of waste properly.
- Soon, political parties realised that if they **promised to improve conditions,** they would get more votes from the working classes. This led to more **public health reforms** being introduced, and marked the end of the laissez-faire attitude towards public health.
- The public health systems were tested by crises such as the **Cattle Plague (1865–1967)** – an outbreak of the **rinderpest virus** that killed over 10% of the cow population in Britain. It had an extremely high mortality rate of 90% and was highly contagious.

Cholera (1831–1866)

- Repeated outbreaks of cholera were a major killer in industrial Britain due to contaminated water supplies.
- It was a fatal disease that caused diarrhoea and vomiting and was nicknamed 'The Blue Death' because extreme dehydration would result in the patient's skin turning grey/blue.

Beliefs about causes	Prevention methods	Treatments	Consequences
• Miasma • Divine punishment • Contagion (though waterborne transmission was not well understood)	• Cleaning streets and removing waste • Avoiding crowds • Smelling vinegar cloths	• Bloodletting • Purging • Opiates • Herbal remedies • Quarantine and isolation (not effective since it was waterborne)	• Tens of thousands of deaths • Public health reforms to improve clean water and sanitation systems

Features of modern Britain

- Economic, political, social, and cultural changes significantly improved living conditions for much of the population in Britain.
- **Housing standards** improved with **council housing projects** and **building regulations** reducing overcrowding and providing indoor plumbing and central heating.
- Diets became more **varied and nutritious**, with increased access to fresh fruit, vegetables, and protein, although the rise of processed foods introduced new health challenges.
- **Air quality** initially worsened due to industrialisation and coal use, leading to **urban smog,** but later pollution control measures, clean air acts, and technological advances reduced respiratory health risks.
- Increasing **mechanisation** and desk-based jobs contributed to **inactivity and obesity,** prompting government campaigns to promote exercise and healthy lifestyles.
- Major innovations are often the product of **collaborations** rather than lone scientists.

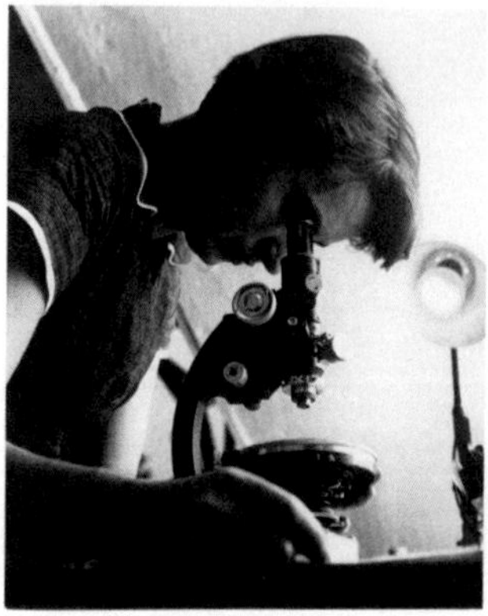

Rosalind Franklin, 1955
MRC Laboratory of Molecular Biology - CC BY-SA 4.0

Modern explanations for illness

- Scientific research in the twentieth and twenty-first centuries revealed the significant influence of **genetic factors** on susceptibility to disease, alongside **lifestyle factors** such as diet, exercise, and smoking.
- New understandings of genetics and the discovery of DNA in 1953, followed by the Human Genome Project in 1990–2003 led to a greater understanding of **hereditary diseases** and the fact that not all diseases are caused by microbes (i.e. some are inherited, such as Down's Syndrome and cystic fibrosis).
- The **pharmaceutical industry** developed rapidly in the twentieth century, enabling the **mass production of effective medicines** for a wide range of illnesses.
- The emergence of new diseases, including **viral infections** and **antibiotic-resistant bacteria,** led to ongoing research and the development of new treatments.

Modern cures and preventions

- **Mass vaccination programmes** became a cornerstone of public health in modern Britain, reducing or eliminating diseases such as polio, measles, and whooping cough.
- **Antibiotics** to treat the growth of bacteria in the body became commonplace. **Penicillin,** discovered by Alexander Fleming in 1928, was a major breakthrough in treating bacterial infections, but it was Florey and Chain who developed methods to produce it for widespread clinical use in the 1940s.
- **Magic bullet** chemicals to kill bacteria rose in popularity after the success of Ehrlich's treatment for syphilis. The second major magic bullet was **Prontosil**, discovered by Gerhard Domagk in 1932 for treating blood poisoning such as streptococcus. This led to the discovery of **sulphonamide** drugs, which treated pneumonia, scarlet fever, and meningitis.
- **Government lifestyle campaigns** addressed public health concerns, promoting exercise, balanced diets, and anti-smoking initiatives, while also introducing measures to reduce environmental pollution.
    - The **Spanish Influenza** pandemic of 1918–19 prompted public health authorities to implement measures such as quarantine, public education, and reporting of infections to control spread.
    - The global **AIDS epidemic,** emerging in the 1980s, required a coordinated response including awareness campaigns, sexual health education, testing programmes, and antiretroviral drugs.
    - **Lung cancer** could be diagnosed with new **CT/PET-CT scans** (detailed body images with dye) and **bronchoscopy** (looking into airways), and PET-CT scans. New treatments included transplants to replace cancerous lungs and radiotherapy/chemotherapy to kill or shrink cancer cells. Research identified smoking as the primary cause of lung cancer, prompting anti-smoking campaigns, legislation on tobacco advertising, and smoking bans in public spaces.
- **Alternative treatments,** such as homeopathy, accupuncture, aromatherapy, and herbal medicine grew in popularity, often alongside mainstream medicine, reflecting a broader understanding of patient choice and holistic care. This includes:
- **Early detection of illnesses,** including cancer and cardiovascular disease, became possible, enhancing treatment outcomes and patient survival rates by improving the accuracy and speed of diagnosis and treatment.

Medical technology in the modern era

Technology	Date	Uses
Radiotherapy	Early 1900s	Using targeted X-rays and gamma rays to kill cancer cells (following the discovery of radiation by Marie Curie, Pierre Curie, and Henri Becquerel). Radiation can be delivered externally or internally (brachytherapy).
Chemotherapy	1940s	Anti-cancer drugs (e.g. nitrogen mustard) circulate in the bloodstream to target rapidly dividing cells and disrupt cell division, slowing or shrinking tumours.
Dialysis and artificial kidneys	1945	An external machine pumps a patient's blood through a machine that diffuses waste products and excess fluid before returning the cleansed blood to the body.
Endoscopy	1950s	Flexible fibre-optic cameras inserted into the body for internal imaging and minimally invasive procedures.
Pacemakers	1952	A device implanted under the skin sends electrical impulses to regulate the heartbeat when the heart's natural rhythm is too slow or irregular.
Transplants	1954	A failing organ is replaced with a compatible donor one. Immunosuppressant drugs prevent rejection.
Ultrasounds	1956	High-frequency sound waves create echoes that translate to non-invasive medical imaging.
CT scans	1971	More advanced form of x-rays used to find tumours with computer-rendered cross-sections of the body.
MRI scans	1973	Uses a strong magnetic field and radio waves to measure atoms in the body and convert them into highly detailed images of soft tissues.
Insulin pumps	1978	Delivers controlled doses of insulin through a catheter into the body, helping people with diabetes maintain stable blood glucose levels without frequent injections.
Keyhole surgery	1980s	Surgeons use long instruments and a camera inserted through a small incision, reducing trauma and recovery time.
Functional MRI (fMRI)	1990s	Measures changes in blood flow and oxygen use to map brain activity during tasks, rather than just anatomy.
Laser surgery	1990s	Focused beams of light cut tissue with high precision, used in eye surgery, dermatology, and tumour removal.
3D printing	2000s	3D printers use bio-ink to construct tissue scaffolds or organ structures to reduce the need for donor organs.

Modern doctors and medical professionals

- Doctors have increasingly **specialised**, reflecting the growing complexity of medical knowledge and technology.
- The discovery of antibiotics, vaccines, and advanced surgical methods drastically **reduced mortality** from infectious diseases.
- Medical practice has become increasingly **evidence-based,** relying on **clinical trials,** standardised protocols, and peer-reviewed research.
- Public health and global health initiatives became central, with doctors playing key roles in outbreak response and health equity.
- Advances in **diagnostic tools,** such as imaging, genetics, and molecular testing, have transformed patient care and early detection.
- Recent innovations, including mRNA vaccines, genomics, and AI, are rapidly reshaping how diseases are diagnosed, treated, and prevented.

Profile: Karl Landsteiner

- Landsteiner discovered the existence of **different blood groups** and Rh factors in 1901.
- He identified that incompatible blood caused dangerous reactions.
- This discovery made **blood transfusions** far safer and led to the development of blood banks and blood donations.
- He also discovered the polio virus and was involved in many key medical research projects throughout the 20th century.

Karl Landsteiner
(b. 1868 d.1943)

Profile: Marie Curie

- Marie Curie was a pioneering scientist who **discovered radioactivity** and was the first person to win Nobel Prizes in both Physics and Chemistry.
- She developed the use of **X-rays for diagnosis** and equip mobile X-ray units for use on WWI battlefields.
- Radiation therapy became important in cancer treatment.
- She died in 1934 from aplastic anaemia, a condition caused by prolonged exposure to high levels of radiation during her research.

Marie Curie
(b. 1867 d.1934)

SNAPREVISE

Profile: Alexander Fleming

- Fleming's accidental discovery of penicillin in 1928 marked the beginning of the antibiotic era, offering the first effective treatment for bacterial infections.
- Penicillin fungal spores had floated into Fleming's lab and landed on a petri dish. Fleming noticed that the mould had killed off harmful *Staphylococcus* bacteria that he was testing.
- However, Fleming did not push for further investigation as he believed it was not a useful discovery in humans and could not develop it fully due to a lack of funding.

Alexander Fleming
(b. 1881 d. 1955)

Profile: Howard Florey and Ernst Chain

- In 1939, Florey and Chain discovered that penicillin killed bacteria in infected mice. They experimented on a local policeman and found the medicine worked well, but the man died when they ran out of penicillin.
- They developed methods for **mass production** of penicillin in the early 1940s, making it widely available to treat infections during and after World War II. However, it took a long period of time to grow enough penicillin for a human.
- By 1941, they had enough penicillin to treat one person.
- **US drug companies** funded mass production, especially after the US entered WWII in 1942, as it saved many wounded soldiers.
- British companies also started mass production in 1943 and would quickly develop enough penicillin to treat **all wounded soldiers** on D-Day in 1944.
- Fleming, Florey, and Chain were all awarded the Nobel Prize in 1945 for their work.
- Penicillin transformed medicine, reducing deaths from otherwise fatal infections and paving the way for the development of more antibiotics.

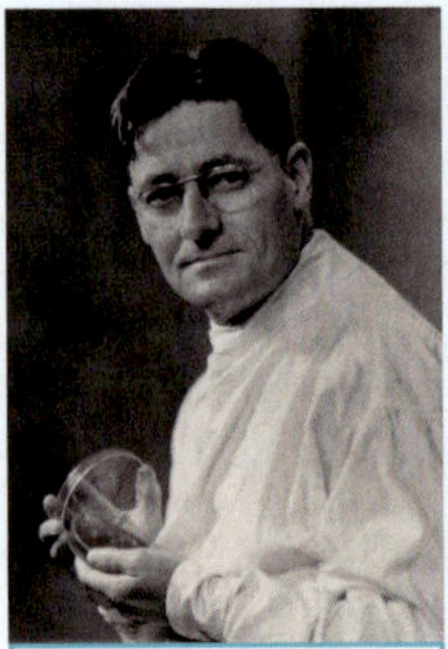

Howard Florey
(b. 1898 d. 1968)

Ernst Chain
(b. 1906 d. 1979)

Modern public health

- **Social reforms:** the Liberal government from 1905–1914 passed a series of reforms to improve public health. This was partly in response to the Boer War where a third of army volunteers were rejected due to poor health.
- Investigations by social reformers such as **Charles Booth** and **Seebohm Rowntree** revealed the extent of poverty in urban areas, highlighting the relationship between socioeconomic conditions and health.
- These reforms included **free school meals** (1906), **medical checks in schools** (1907), the **National Insurance Act** (1911), and the **Clean Air Act** (1956 and 1968).
- The **Beveridge Report of 1944** recommended comprehensive social welfare reforms, leading to the creation of the Welfare State, which aimed to eliminate the 'five giants' negatively impacting people's lives.

Five Giants	New Labour response
Want	Providing benefits to the poor
Disease	Establishing the NHS in 1948
Ignorance	Raising the school leaving age to 15
Squalor	Slum clearance programmes
Idleness	Weekly family allowances

- **The National Health Service (NHS),** established in 1948 by Aneurin Bevan (Minister for Health), provided **free healthcare at the point of use,** paid for by National Insurance contributions. This greatly improved access to treatment regardless of income.
  - Before the NHS, healthcare was expensive and highly limited. This was evidenced by high infant mortality rates.
  - The combination of the NHS, modern pharmaceuticals, high-tech hospital treatment, and innovations like antibiotics and vaccines represents one of the most significant periods of change in healthcare in British history, offering a level of **care and prevention unimaginable in previous eras.**
  - In the long-term, life expectancy increased, which has caused strains on the NHS. In the twenty-first century, public healthcare faces challenges including rising costs, choices regarding treatment options, and **pressures on NHS resources** due to an ageing population and chronic illness prevalence.

Innovations from WWI

- **Blood transfusions:** Karl Landsteiner's discovery of blood groups helped doctors realise that a transfusion only worked when the blood was matched. However, it was difficult to store blood for long. In 1914, Albert Hustein found that storing blood with sodium made it last longer, enabling it to be transported to battlefields. The national blood transfusion service opened in 1938. This was supported by large blood banks that took donations from the public.
- **X-rays:** first invented by Wilhelm Roentgen in 1895, these allowed doctors to view inside the body and locate bullets or shrapnel. Early machines were large, slow (90 minutes per x-ray), and gave off high radiation, so smaller mobile x-ray machines were developed for use on the battlefield.
- **Plastic surgery:** Harold Gillies set up a skin graft clinic for soldiers with severe facial injuries. Gillies and his men treated over 5000 soldiers by 1921. Later, in WWII, Archibald McIndoe (a cousin of Harold Gillies) began using penicillin to prevent infection during plastic surgeries.
- **Treatment of infections:** through a lot of trial and error, surgeons found that cutting away infected flesh (debridement) and soaking it in saline solution was the best prevention from infection spreading. The **Carrel-Dakin method (1917)** used sterilised salt solution to clean wounds, as carbolic acid was ineffective against gas gangrene.
- **Amputation:** by 1918, 240,000 men had lost limbs, so surgeons were proficient in this procedure and utilised new methods of sterilisation and antiseptic techniques to reduce the risk of infections or complications.
- **Leg splints:** the Thomas splint or army leg splint was developed during WWI to treat broken legs by stabilising and elevating them to help them heal and reduce the need for amputation. Robert Jones taught medics how to use it in 1915, and survival rates for leg injuries increased from 20% to 82%. Improved versions of these leg splints are still used today.

Trench warfare

- **Frontline trench:** where attacks were launched and most fighting occurred.
- **Support trench:** located about 80 meters behind the frontline; used for retreat and support.
- **Reserve trench:** about 100 meters behind the support trench; troops stationed here for counterattacks.
- **Dugouts:** holes in the side of trenches for soldiers to take cover.
- **Zig-zag design:** trenches were built in zigzags to limit the impact of explosions and shrapnel.
- **Artillery emplacements:** used to launch explosives over long distances.

Injuries and illnesses from the trenches

- **Shell shock:** psychological trauma from constant bombardment. Symptoms included tiredness, nightmares, tremors, and mental breakdowns. Some soldiers were evacuated to hospitals but others were accused of cowardice even when unable to speak, move, or stay still. Eventually, there were so many cases of shell shock that it was officially recognised. Today, it is known as a form of post-traumatic stress disorder (PTSD).
- **Trench fever:** caused by lice; symptoms included flu-like illness, headaches, fever, and aching muscles. Delousing stations were set up in 1918 to help prevent and treat it.
- **Shrapnel injuries:** caused by bullets or fragments from explosions. Metal pieces could penetrate the body, causing severe internal damage and infection. Steel Brodie helmets were introduced to protect soldiers' heads.
- **Trench foot:** caused by standing in cold, wet trenches for long periods. Symptoms included painful swelling and gangrene, sometimes leading to amputation. Prevention included rubbing whale oil on feet, keeping feet dry, changing socks, and using duckboards and pumps to drain water.
- **Gas attacks:** chlorine, phosgene, and mustard gas caused burning, blisters, and suffocation. Psychological impact included fear and panic. Gas masks were developed in 1915 to protect soldiers.
- **Gas gangrene:** caused by bacteria infecting open wounds, often from soil. Symptoms included dead tissue and gas build-up in wounds. Treatment usually involved amputation.

Treatment in the trenches

- **Stretcher bearers** collected and carried wounded men to the first stage of treatment.
- **Royal Army Medical Corps (RAMC):** army branch responsible for medical care, founded in 1898.
- **First Aid Nursing Yeomanry (FANY):** women's organisation founded in 1907. They sent women to the Western Front to support medical services, drive ambulances, and provide first aid and food.
- **Regimental Aid Posts (RAP):** provided immediate first aid, aiming to return as many men as possible to the front line. They could not treat serious injuries but were often located in communication trenches for rapid response.
- **Advanced Dressing Stations (ADS)** and **Main Dressing Stations (MDS):** treated more serious injuries. They were in abandoned buildings, bunkers, or tents. They were staffed by RAMC field ambulance units, which could treat 150 patients or thousands during major battles.
- **Casualty Clearing Stations (CCS):** dealt with the most critical injuries. They set up in buildings like factories and schools, further from the frontline. They also used a **triage** system: wounded soldiers who could walk were returned to the front, those needing hospital were sent to base, and those with no chance of survival were made comfortable.
- **Base hospitals:** performed the most serious operations and were located near the coast for easy evacuation to Britain. They were divided into wards with specialist doctors.
- **Underground hospital at Arras (Nov 1916):** built in tunnels and caves under Arras, known as Thomas Cave. It had 700 beds, waiting rooms, an operating theatre, a mortuary, electricity, and piped water.

Summary table

SNAPREVISE

	Cures and prevention	Surgery	Public health
War	**Industrial:** Franco-Prussian rivalry between Pasteur and Koch **Modern:** WWII funding of penicillin	**Modern:** WWI and WWII advancements **Renaissance:** Paré stress of saving lives	**Modern:** war revealed poor health (e.g. Boer war rejections)
Religion	**Medieval**: Islamic spread of knowledge **Renaissance:** decline in religious authority led to more scientific approaches	**Medieval**: dissection discouraged by the Church; monasteries provided clean environments	**Medieval:** the church provided some aid during the plagues **Renaissance**: closing of monasteries allowed for the hospital
Individuals	**Medieval:** Galen **Industrial:** Pasteur, Koch, Jenner **Modern:** Fleming, Beveridge	**Renaissance:** Pare, Vesalius **Industrial:** Lister, Simpson **Modern:** Gillies	**Industrial:** Chadwick, Snow, Bazalgette **Modern:** Beveridge and Bevan
Government	**Industrial:** laissez faire originally but later funded research (Pasteur) **Modern:** supported antibiotic production and health campaigns	**Modern:** funded medical training	**Industrial:** public health acts, Great Stink **Modern:** NHS, welfare state
Funding	**Industrial:** initially poor funding; later government invested in Germ Theory. **Modern:** US & UK wartime investment allowed penicillin production; NHS funded via National Insurance	**Industrial:** carbolic acid expensive and unpopular. **Modern:** NHS made surgery more accessible, but rising costs put pressure on resources	**Industrial:** poverty in cities worsened slum conditions; Chadwick's report **Modern:** welfare state aimed to reduce long-term costs through improved health
Science and technology	**Renaissance:** the printing press spread ideas. **Industrial:** microscopes allowed Koch to identify specific bacteria; telegraph spread findings	**Industrial:** antiseptics, chloroform as anesthetic **Modern:** MRI, CT scans, blood transfusions, heart surgery, prosthetics	**Industrial:** sewer systems, improved water supplies. **Modern:** public health databases, national screening programs, advanced diagnostics (e.g. DNA analysis)